Flavio Roberto Bueno de Camargo

Promoting the use of the Virtual Learning Environment

Flavio Roberto Bueno de Camargo

Promoting the use of the Virtual Learning Environment

Study on teachers' non-adoption and under-utilisation of educational technology

ScienciaScripts

Imprint

Any brand names and product names mentioned in this book are subject to trademark, brand or patent protection and are trademarks or registered trademarks of their respective holders. The use of brand names, product names, common names, trade names, product descriptions etc. even without a particular marking in this work is in no way to be construed to mean that such names may be regarded as unrestricted in respect of trademark and brand protection legislation and could thus be used by anyone.

Cover image: www.ingimage.com

This book is a translation from the original published under ISBN 978-613-9-72373-7.

Publisher:
Sciencia Scripts
is a trademark of
Dodo Books Indian Ocean Ltd. and OmniScriptum S.R.L publishing group

120 High Road, East Finchley, London, N2 9ED, United Kingdom
Str. Armeneasca 28/1, office 1, Chisinau MD-2012, Republic of Moldova, Europe
Printed at: see last page
ISBN: 978-620-7-94056-1

SUMMARY

The use of Virtual Learning Environments (VLEs) in higher education institutions aims to modernise and add value to the teaching and learning process. Thus, after 14 years of using various VLEs, the Getulio Vargas Foundation (FGV) decided to implement a single VLE for its eight schools. The challenge of implementation was handled with a great deal of planning and relied on the advantages of the new environment, as well as a simple strategy of intense communication and training for teachers. Despite the efforts made, some teachers are not using the new platform or are using it only superficially. The aim of this study is to analyse the rate of use of this platform. It also aims to identify the critical points of the lack of take-up by teachers. As a result of this work, the assumptions that lead to an understanding of the suitability of the system were reviewed, as well as the development of an action plan that contributes to increasing adherence to the new tool.

Key words: Virtual Learning Environment; Communication and Training; Implementation of Educational Technology; Adherence.

SUMMARY

CHAPTER 1

INTRODUCTION

The use of educational technologies, specifically Virtual Learning Environments (VLE) at the Getulio Vargas Foundation (FGV) is not new. FGV, through its schools and the online FGV Executive Education Programme, has been bringing innovation to the market for over 20 years, not only by offering courses and subjects entirely online, but mainly by using educational technologies to support face-to-face teaching and learning.

FGV brings together eight schools with different characteristics in two major cities, Rio de Janeiro and São Paulo, and until December 2014 had four Virtual Learning Environments (VLE), with five schools sharing the same VLE and three others with little experience and/or unsuccessful experiences in using VLE.

At the end of 2014, after extensive market research, a new VLE was purchased. The new VLE, whose original name was *Brightspace,* was implemented, but it was decided to call it the new ECLASS so as not to be linked to the commercial name. This new name alludes to one of the old VLEs that was more widespread at FGV.

This implementation involved intensive homologation involving technicians, analysts, teaching staff and other strategically selected agents, as well as communication and training workshops to meet all the needs of users of the new platform.

As a result, at the beginning of 2015 the new ECLASS was implemented in all eight FGV schools, and the four previous systems were officially switched off. It's important to note that at least two of them had been consolidated for 12 years.

1.1 Presentation of the problem, the objective and its relevance

The problem to be solved and which guides this case study was described as follows: "Non-adherence to the use of ECLASS and its under-utilisation by a portion of the teaching staff at the Getulio Vargas Foundation". Faced with this problem, this study sought to identify its possible causes and present possible suggestions for solutions.

The aim of this study is to analyse the rate of use of the ECLASS platform by FGV lecturers. In addition, it aims to identify the critical points of the lack of adherence by teachers. As a result of this work, the assumptions that lead to an understanding of the suitability of the system were reviewed, as well as the development of an action plan that contributes to increasing adherence to the new tool. Given the situation identified in Figures 1.1 and 1.2, which indicate a high rate of use of ECLASS after its implementation, it is also possible to see that there is still a proportion of FGV lecturers who do not use it. The statistical research methodology, a field of applied statistics, will be applied to empirically confirm the non-adherence of a portion of the teaching staff to the new tool and to test hypotheses for the factors that influenced this portion of the teaching staff not to adhere to the ECLASS system.

1.2 Company presentation

The context of this work takes place at the Getúlio Vargas Foundation, a non-profit private law institution that operates in the education sector. FGV was founded on 20 December 1944 with the aim of promoting the intellectual and technical development of the human contingent, thus creating an internationally competitive and sustainable Brazil. In order to achieve this goal, FGV has reference higher education schools as well as valuable documentation and research centres.

Throughout its existence, FGV has offered technical advice to organisations to promote their business progress.

FGV's academic establishment is on a par with the most developed educational institutions in the world, and it also has exchange agreements with many of these institutions.

FGV is a reference in education in Brazil, and is recognised internationally for the various programmes it offers, such as undergraduate, specialisation, master's and doctoral courses, as well as the technical assistance it offers in the form of consultancy.

As one of the most important centres of excellence, FGV always strives to be an innovative institution, providing its students and society as a whole with a unique educational experience.

FGV is an organisation that looks at the world in search of the modern. Looking for what can be beneficial and appropriate for Brazil's progress, thus building a more virtuous and evolved country.

Its audience is made up of young students, professionals and executives who crave the most refined knowledge. With this in mind, FGV always endeavours to bring the latest to its schools by using educational technologies.

Access to the internet is becoming an increasingly frequent habit and, according to a survey carried out by CETIC (Centre for Studies on Information and Communication Technologies), the number of connected Brazilian homes reached 32.3 million in 2014. In view of this, FGV realised that its students now have greater access to information than those who relied exclusively on libraries and few technological resources.

This development extends to courses, programmes and activities that accompany the evolution of corporations and their needs in terms of professional qualification and specialisation.

In turn, FGV's audience is gradually becoming more and more immersed in interactive technologies, and as a result FGV has faced the challenge of adapting its andragogical activities to new educational technologies.

One of the tools incorporated by FGV is the Virtual Learning Environment (VLE). Within FGV, the AVA is responsible for managing and creating virtual classrooms, i.e. it is an extension of the face-to-face classroom. This allows teachers to make content available in a single place in an organised way, as well as providing tests and other activities so that students can learn autonomously, with quality and from anywhere with internet access.

The VLE has become a more comprehensive and important technology for the academic routine, as it is creating new platforms that can be accessed via mobile, allowing teaching to reach students' technological devices at all times when teaching is needed.

The dynamics provided by this system are very satisfactory for distance learning, since it provides an educational and essentially technological environment, generating greater integration with the teachers and students involved.

By using these technologies, FGV is increasingly seeking to increase its efficiency, effectiveness and competitiveness in relation to its competitors.

1.3 Hypotheses

According to Luna (1997), based on analyses of the available knowledge, the researcher ends up "betting" on what might emerge as a result of their research. Once the problem has been formulated, a supposed, probable and provisional answer is proposed, which would be what the researcher believes to be plausible as a solution to the problem. That said, below are the supposed answers to the problem already reported:

1. Older teachers may use ECLASS less.
2. Teachers with more time on the job may use ECLASS less.
3. Teachers with more time on the job are also older teachers.
4. Teachers from a particular school may use ECLASS less.
5. The lack of take-up and under-utilisation may have been due to a lack of communication and publicity about the platform and its benefits;
6. The perception of benefits is directly related to the teachers' awareness of the existing functionalities.

1.4 Justification for the work

According to the data and graphs below, it can be seen that the use of the new ECLASS has been widespread. However, there is a proportion of teachers who have not joined or who underuse the VLE. This information provides a comparative picture of teachers' use of the new ECLASS, broken down by school, from 2015 to 2016.

Table 1 - Utilisation data for the new ECLASS

TEACHERS AT D2L							
	2015			2016			Accession 2016 compared to the same period in 2015
School	Total Lyceum on 04/03/15	Teachers at D2L on 04/03/15	Accession 04/03/15	Total Lyceum on 17/03/16	Teachers at D2L on 17/03/2016	Accession 17/03/16	
EAESP	289	30	10%	239	212	89%	78%
EESP	128	5	4%	70	55	79%	75%
LAW SP	188	54	29%	86	67	78%	49%
EBAPE	103	2	2%	51	37	73%	71%
EMAp	32	4	13%	14	8	57%	45%
CPDOc	48	9	19%	37	6	16%	-3%
RJ LAW	68	5	7%	52	12	23%	16%
EPGE	25	0	0%	31	6	19%	19%
TOTAL	881	109	12%	580	403	69%	57%

Source: author's elaboration

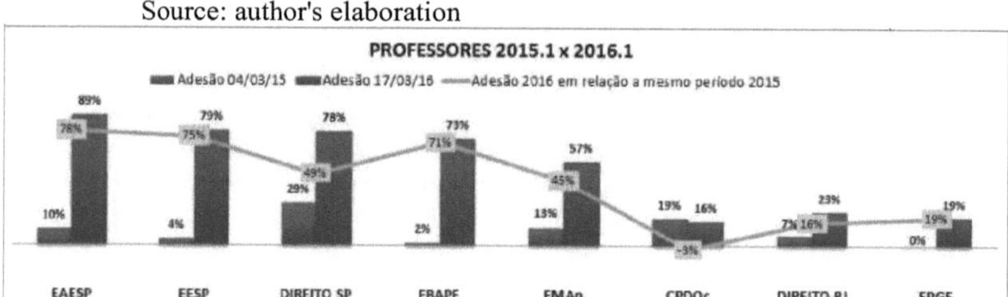

Graph 1 - Graph with data on the use of the new ECLASS Source: author's work

Given this data, there is a need for action to increase adherence to the use of ECLASS, especially in units with a rate below 50%. FGV aims to win over this portion of teachers who still don't use ECLASS, and this study will contribute to the measures needed to achieve this goal.

1.5 Organising the report

This work analyses the methods taught in the Statistics subject that forms part of the curriculum of the Specialisation Course in Administration for Graduates (CEAG).

One of these methods adopted is the correlation of information, which is one of the methods used to develop the research that guides this project. This method will prove the problem identified, which is "non-adherence to and under-utilisation of educational technology by teachers", as well as providing tools for applying an action/decision plan that will be discussed at the end of this study. It is therefore worth pointing out here that research will be a great ally of this study.

"Statistical science provides widely used tools to infer results from a database, which may contain qualitative or quantitative information, with different means of collecting information and demonstrating the data" (MARTINS; DOMINGUES, 2014).

"In general, many of the authors in this area demonstrate their results through graphs, charts and tables with the data obtained, accompanied by descriptive statistics (averages, standard deviations, medians) and almost always mentioning the statistical tests carried out" (LAKATOS; MARCONI, 2010).

Knowledge of basic statistical concepts is therefore essential in order to avoid some common mistakes. Among these important concepts are the definition of a variable and its classifications.

"We can define a variable as the characteristic that is measured or evaluated in each element of the sample" (RUMSEY, 2009).

Variables can have numeric or non-numeric values and are classified as follows:

Table 2 - Definition of Quantitative and Qualitative Variables

Quantitative variables	These are characteristics that can be described by number: Continuous: is evaluated in numbers that are the result of measurements and, therefore, can take on values with decimal places and must be measured by means of an instrument. Discrete: is evaluated in numbers that are the result of counting and therefore only integers make sense.
Qualitative or Categorical Variables	These are characteristics that do not have quantitative values, but instead are defined by categories, i.e. they represent a classification of individuals. They can be Nominal: there is no ordering of the categories. Examples: sex, eye colour, smoker/non-smoker, sick/sad. Ordinal: there is an ordering between the categories. Examples: schooling (1st, 2nd° , 3rd° grades), stage of illness (initial, intermediate, terminal), month of observation (January, February, March...).

Source: RUMSEY, 2009.

Note: Adapted by the author.

However, the distinctions are less rigid than the above description implies. An originally quantitative variable can be collected qualitatively. For example, the variable age, measured in complete years, is quantitative (continuous); but if only the age range is reported (0 to 5 years, 6 to 10 years, etc...), it is qualitative (ordinal).

The research is therefore based on these concepts and the most important methodological challenges include making a decision in the form of the flowchart below:

Table 3 - Definition of the researcher's decision-making steps

1	Determine needs / problems
2	Drawing up and evaluating the questionnaire
3	Determine sampling
4	Apply questionnaire
5	Analysing data
6	Conclusion/ Improvement plan

Source: author's elaboration

Following the researcher's conceptual decision-making criteria, the work was planned as follows:

1. The key points that would justify the non-adherence to ECLASS by a proportion of FGV teachers were identified.

2. The existing resources of the new ECLASS were surveyed, which would make it possible to measure the under-utilisation of the virtual learning environment.

3. The questionnaire was structured by establishing the questions and response alternatives, so that a statistical analysis could later be carried out to solve the problem.

4. The questionnaire was created in the Google Forms tool.

5. The survey was publicised and applied to all the teachers at the eight FGV schools. The dissemination was consolidated via institutional e-mail by the area responsible for administering ECLASS, which is the Educational Technologies Coordination (CTE), thus strengthening the incentive for all teachers to respond to the questionnaire, thereby contributing to improvements in the new system.

6. The results of the survey will be disseminated to teachers and their coordinators. In addition, the information will be used to strategically reorganise and draw up an action plan to resolve the problems raised in this study.

CHAPTER 2

OBSERVING THE ORGANISATION'S REALITY

We are living in a time when formal education, intellect, information and knowledge are becoming universal. In Brazil, higher education is booming and this is creating many challenges for institutions, especially traditional ones like FGV.

There is a high growth in the number of higher education courses on offer and a high level of competition in this market. With the spread of distance learning, competition has become fiercer, forcing institutions to be more competitive and to reinvent themselves.

We are living in an information and knowledge society that places great importance on the key role that information and its consequent evolution play. This issue has become a paradigm in many fields of human endeavour. However, despite the fact that the idea that intellectual capital and knowledge are the differentiating factors between failure and success has already been widely explored, there is still much to discuss on the subject.

Currently, with the creation of technical-scientific knowledge on the increase, a significant portion of symbolic exchanges take place within the field of andragogy, which is understood as the art or science of guiding adults to learn (KNOWLES, 1973). In other words, most of the time knowledge is created and disseminated in higher education institutions where andragogy takes place in its entirety.

Not so long ago, an adult with higher education was considered a differential, but nowadays higher education is considered a prerequisite. The reason why continuous learning is so important is that it is well known that in the social and professional spheres, knowledge becomes obsolete in a short space of time. Knowledge is often unable to last for more than one generation, so much so that only a small part of a person's life can be devoted to the learning process. This process needs to be lengthened, because knowledge spans a lifetime, forcing us to always be learning.

The tendency is for individuals to be in constant contact with education and training practices throughout their lives, incessantly searching for updates that will enable them to relate better to the full potential of life. The world is increasingly demanding such complexity.

The social and economic development of a globalised world depends on human capital that is prepared and educated, and these are consequences that have occurred everywhere. The role of higher education institutions, such as FGV, is necessary for continuous learning to take place. Such institutions can promote the necessary constant updating of the human intellect by being a great incubator and disseminator of knowledge. Such is their importance that the following pages have been devoted to discussing the role of the FGV, the use of educational technologies at the FGV and the importance of using technologies in HEIs, as well as the higher education scenario in Brazil and some important data about the FGV.

2.1 The use of educational technologies at FGV

The Getulio Vargas Foundation has consolidated experience in using technology to support its many processes and areas of activity. It uses it to develop programmes used primarily for administrative processes, but above all it uses it to support education, its main service. As already mentioned, FGV had 4 different types of virtual learning environments to support face-to-face classes and distance learning.

A VLE enables different ways of learning and teaching through the use of digital and interactive technologies. The main objectives of using a VLE in a HEI are to develop new teaching methodologies and expand communication between students and teachers, all centred and organised in the same place.

The VLE allows teachers to create an extension of the classroom, thus organising the virtual environment according to their needs, and it can contain: teaching content and activities, a detailed programme of lessons, bibliographies, methodology, support materials, assessment, tests, links, surveys, discussion forums, a tool for checking plagiarism, group management, among other various resources.

In this way, the teacher can use the time during face-to-face meetings in the classroom to encourage interactivity between students, develop new teaching methodologies and work on group dynamics, thus leaving different situations for face-to-face meetings that the VLE does not allow for.

Collaboration and communication resources are powerful tools for interaction between the various users of a VLE. For Carvalho (2010), in addition to interaction tools, assessment and interactive communication tools are the most important features of a VLE. But in a VLE you can find many other functionalities, such as those presented below:

Table 4 - LMS Functionality Characteristics

Individual Work Functionality	*Interaction and Communication Functionality*
Monitoring activities	Interactive 3D environment
Online activities and games	Student area
Self-evaluation	Audio conferencing
Notepad	Blog
Operational control	Text chat
Access functionality	Instant communicator
Return functionalities	Learning communities

Glossary
History of activities
Languages
General information
External links
List of participants
Downloadable material
Search engines
Personalisation

Internal email
Fun
FAQ help
Smart FAQ
Discussion forums
M-learning
Multimedia
Mural
Student profile
Virtual classroom
Video conferencing
Whiteboard
Wiki

Source: Carvalho (2010)

Despite all the features available, in practice, the VLE may not be being used to the full, as one of the hypotheses raised in this study suggests, and so it may not be providing the paradigm shift necessary for the current teaching and learning process.

According to several authors such as Arvan, 2009; Cuban, 2001; Lane, 2009; US Department of Education, 2010, the use of VLE is alarming, because VLE serves as an affirmation of traditional teaching in the digital environment. The teacher is not opposed to the VLE, and the student only gains the benefit of the convenience of electronic file distribution, as any other cloud service could offer such a service. According to these authors, VLEs do not meet the new demands of student-centred teaching, as they work in a content-centred way.

However, the VLE is just one of the technologies used by FGV. There are also educational technologies that enable distance learning through videoconferencing, the collaborative creation of texts, the exchange and dissemination of knowledge through asynchronous discussions and debates, among many other technologies. What we have seen at FGV and at other HEIs around the world is that more and more educational technology solutions are being integrated into a single environment, which is why it is so important to have a robust VLE that meets the different learning needs.

As mentioned in previous chapters, when selecting a single VLE for the FGV, a study was carried out of all the major suppliers on the market, including the possibility of developing and managing a VLE created by the FGV. After extensive research, the choice was made to adopt Brightspace, a VLE supplied by the Canadian company Desire to Learn.

This VLE is robust and has a wide range of resources that support learning, such as those mentioned above, videoconferences, wikis, which are for creating collaborative texts, discussion forums, quizzes for creating self-correcting tests, which saves teachers time, and the possibility of checking for plagiarism in work sent through the system. Having said this, it can be said that the use of a VLE tends to bring real gains for FGV, which currently has 31,200 users on ECLASS dedicated to the eight schools, plus 107,800 users on the IDE's ECLASS, which is mostly dedicated to online courses.

2.2 Scenario of the higher education sector in Brazil

In order to analyse the sector in which the Getulio Vargas Foundation is located, data from the 2015 Higher Education Census, released in 2017 by the Anísio Teixeira National Institute for Educational Studies and Research (INEP), was analysed. This data provides important information on how higher education is developed and organised in Brazil.

All the data provides a complete overview of higher education in Brazil, but this study will consider the most important data in this sector. As mentioned above, this information is based on data published by the 2015 Census of Higher Education in Brazil.

Higher education institutions (HEIs) in Brazil are university centres, colleges, universities and technical schools (Federal Institutes and Cefets), separated in terms of their administrative category (public or private). Note that private institutions, such as the Getulio Vargas Foundation, have a much higher number of HEIs than public institutions. Note in the graph below that 87.5 per cent are private institutions.

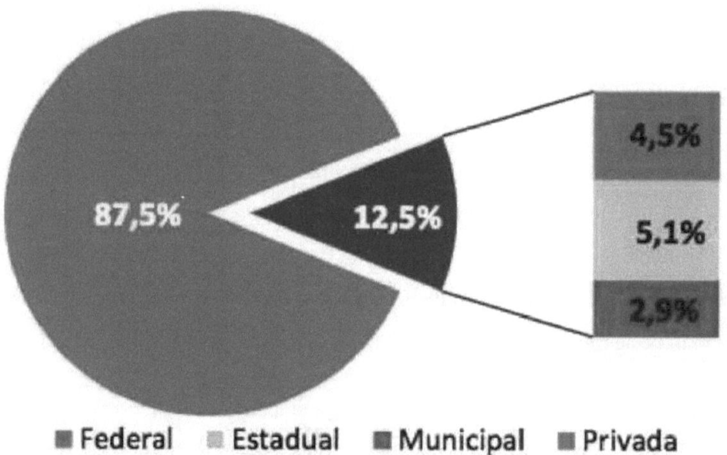

Graph 2 - Percentage of Higher Education Institutions by administrative category

Source: INEP - Higher Education Census 2015

There were 2,364 HEIs in Brazil in 2015, comprising 2,069 private institutions and 295 public ones. It is noteworthy that in the last 15 years there has been exponential growth to the point of doubling the number of HEIs. The growth was 106 per cent in the private sector and 68 per cent in the public sector. However, the higher education sector shrank by 0.2 per cent in 2015.

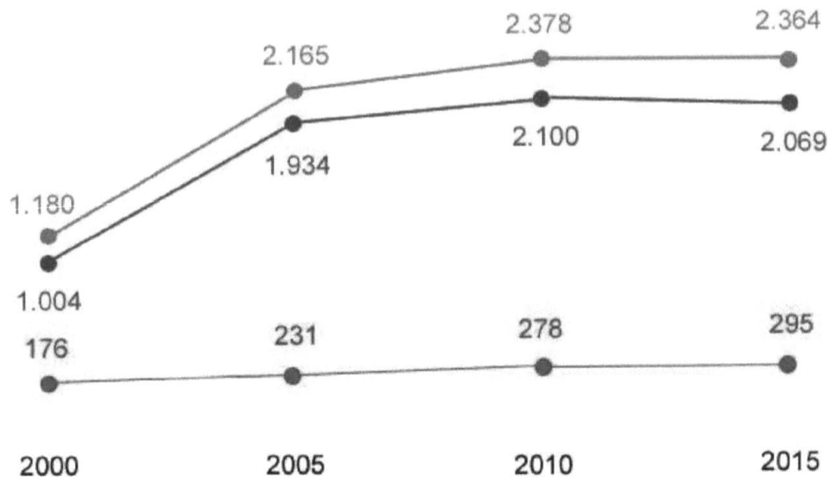

Graph 3 - Higher education institutions in Brazil

Source: INEP - Higher Education Census 2015

Since 2005, the number of enrolments in undergraduate courses has been growing steadily. With the Reuni programme for the expansion and restructuring of federal universities, the public network has seen an increase in places in recent years, but the private network has the largest number of undergraduate students. In 2015 alone, it accounted for 75% of undergraduate enrolments. With the development of programmes such as Prouni (University for All Programme) and FIES (Student Financing Fund), which are grants for low-income students and subsidised financing, the increase in the number of enrolments in the private higher education network is justified.

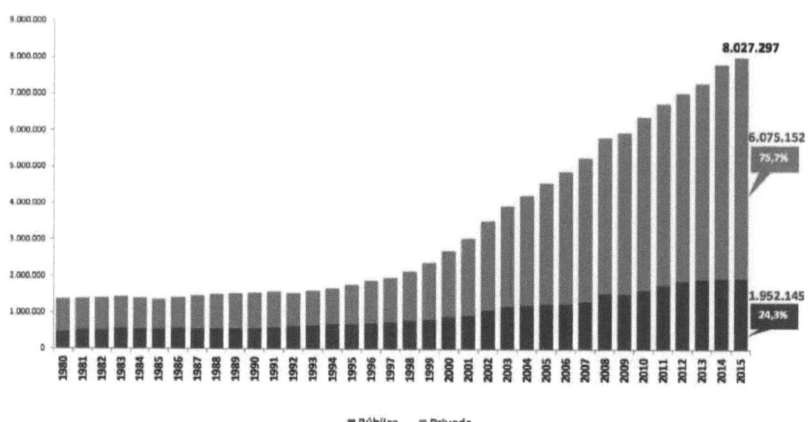

Graph 4 - Enrolment in undergraduate programmes by administrative category (1980-2015)

Source: INEP - Higher Education Census 2015

When it comes to major fields of study, the majority of enrolments are in law, business, social sciences, followed by education. The average in the countries of the Organisation for Cooperation and Development is much better distributed among the main areas, and note that the discrepancy is not so significant in the percentage of students who chose engineering, science, production and construction, computing and mathematics. Analysing the number of graduates, see table below, however, shows the discrepancy. If we consider an average period of 5 years for an undergraduate student to graduate, Brazil has the capacity to graduate less than half of the entrants who choose the two major areas. The table below also allows us to see the evolution in the number of enrolments in all areas from 2010 to 2015.

Table 5 - Number of admissions and graduates in undergraduate programmes per 10,000 inhabitants, according to general subject area OECD countries 2014 compared to Brazil 2010-2015

General Course Area	Ingresses per 10,000 inhabitants							Completed for every 10,000 inhabitants						
	OECD	Brazil						OECD	Brazil					
	2014	2010	2011	2012	2013	2014	2015	2014	2010	2011	2012	2013	2014	2015
Social sciences, business and law	21,7	47,1	50,3	59,7	56,4	61,3	55,8	23,2	21,6	22,0	23,1	21,8	22,1	24,3
Education	5,1	23,7	23,3	24,8	23,6	28,0	25,9	5,4	12,2	12,2	11,3	10,0	10,7	11,6
Health and wellbeing	9.8	14,3	14,3	16,4	17,0	20,4	19,7	9.8	7,5	7,8	8,2	7,0	6,7	7,7
Engineering, production and construction	11.5	12,3	) 14,8	19,0	20,2	22,7	20,8	9.1	3,1	3,3	3,8	4,0	4,4	
Science, maths and computing	5,9	8,5	) 8,2	9.1	8.9	9.3	8,9	5,7	2,9	2,9	3,0	2,7	2,8	3,0
Agriculture and veterinary science	1.2	2,2	2,3	2,7	2.8	3,3	3,3	1,1	1,0	1,0	1,0	1,0	1,0	1,1

| Humanities and arts | 10,9 | 2,8 | 3,0 | 3,4 | 3,3 | 3,3 | 3,4 | 11,4 | 1,2 | 1,3 | 1,4 | 1,4 | 1,4 | 1,4 |
| Services | | 4,8 | 3,1 | 3,4 | 3,9 | 4,2 | 4,1 | 4,1 | 4.8 | 1,6 | 1,5 | 1,6 | 1,4 | 1,6 | 1,9 |

Source: INEP - Higher Education Census 2015.

Higher education institutions are seeing an increase in the number of teachers with master's degrees and doctorates. It's worth noting that the data in the graph below shows that public institutions are mostly made up of professors with a doctorate, while private institutions have the highest proportion of teachers with a master's degree, which shows us that academic production is possibly concentrated in public institutions.

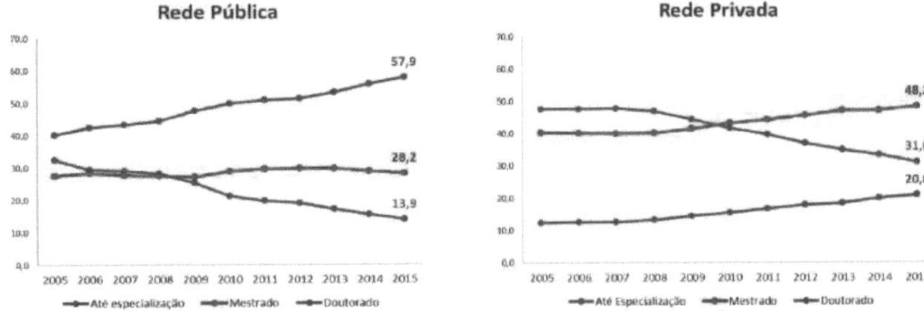

Graph 5 - Proportion of public and private undergraduate higher education teachers by degree level (2005-2015)

Source: INEP - Higher Education Census 2015

Below you'll find an analysis of some relevant indices on the education panorama in August 2017, available from SEMESP:

Table 6 - SEMESP indices

		ISI (ÍNDICE SEMESP DE INGRESSANTES)	ISM (ÍNDICE SEMESP DE MATRÍCULAS)	ISP (ÍNDICE SEMESP DE PROCURA)
PRESENCIAL	2016	1,64 🔽	4,69 🔽	-21,0%
	2017	1,72 🔼	4,88 🔼	-1,9%
EAD	2016	0,82 🔼	1,37 🔼	2,2%
	2017	0,83 🔼	1,46 🔼	10,3%

Source: SEMESP - Analysis of August/2017 indices

The graph below shows estimates of the number of entrants to face-to-face courses at private higher education institutions, according to the survey carried out up to August 2017.

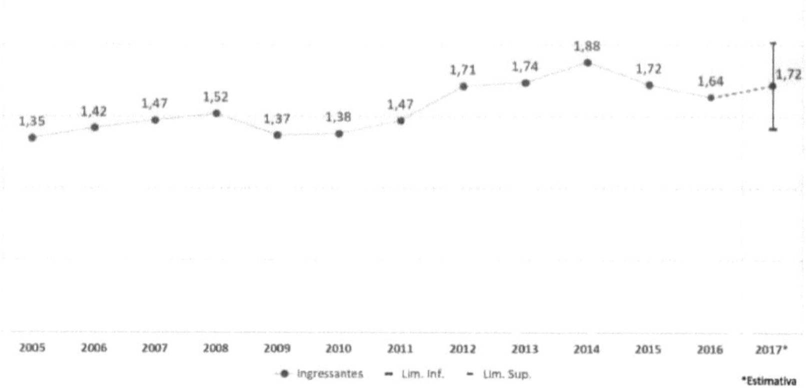

Graph 6 - Entrants to On-Campus Courses in the Private Network - Brazil (in millions) Source: SEMESP - Analysis of August/2017 indices

The chart below shows estimates of the number of entrants to distance learning courses at private higher education institutions, according to the survey carried out up to August 2017.

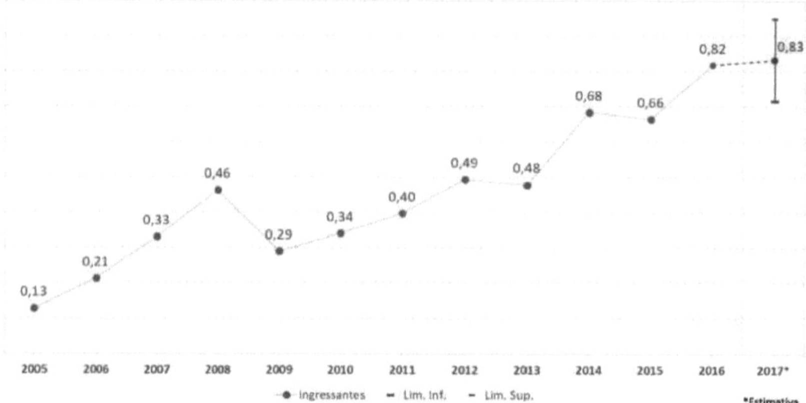

Graph 7 - Private Distance Learning Course Entrants - Brazil (in millions)
Source: SEMESP - Analysis of August/2017 indices

The graph below shows the estimated number of enrolments in face-to-face courses at private higher education institutions according to the survey carried out up to August 2017.

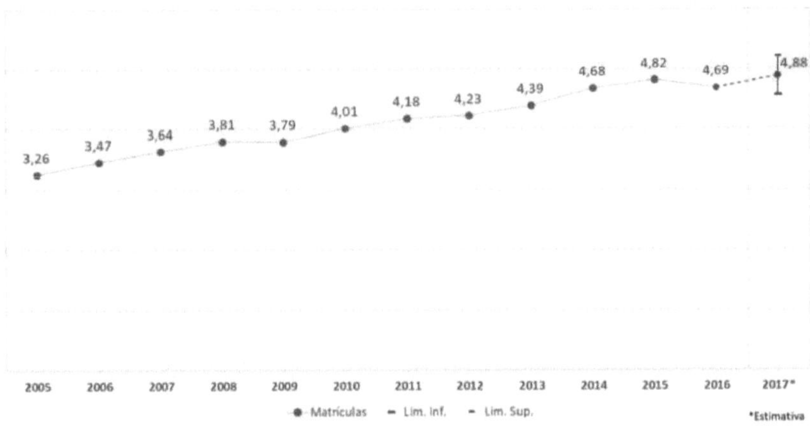

Graph 8 - Enrolment in face-to-face courses Private Network - Brazil (in millions)

Source: SEMESP - Analysis of August/2017 indices

The graph below shows the estimated number of enrolments in distance learning courses at private higher education institutions according to the survey carried out up to August 2017.

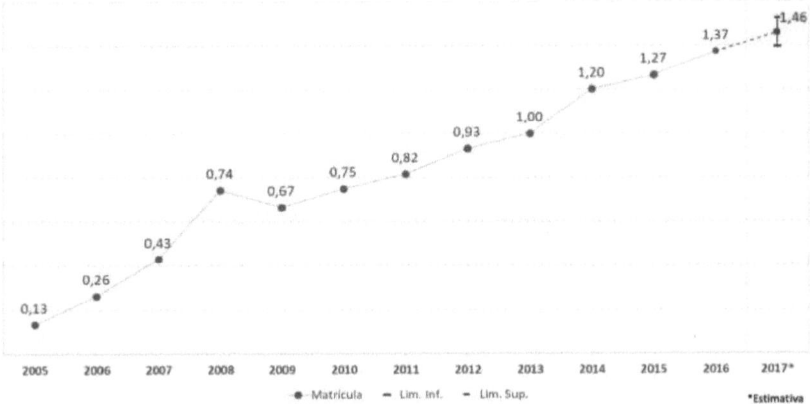

Graph 9 - Enrolment in distance learning courses Private Network - Brazil (in millions) Source: SEMESP - Analysis of August/2017 indices

2.3 Problem and opportunity

Although the Getulio Vargas Foundation's eight schools use the ECLASS virtual learning environment as a support platform for face-to-face courses, it may be that in the future this same VLE will be adopted for distance learning courses offered by the schools. This makes it necessary for teachers to be aware of and fully master the potential offered by ECLASS.

This kind of knowledge will help FGV to become more competitive with its competitors who already use VLEs in their courses. There is currently a trend towards the use of distance education tools and resources that support learning. Note that students themselves often ask their teachers to use ECLASS in their courses.

Teachers who don't adhere to the use of this powerful resource fail to contribute to the foundation as a whole, either by not facilitating student learning or by failing to optimise tasks that could be carried out via ECLASS.

This study will seek to understand what causes these teachers not to join ECLASS and what actions can be taken to change this situation.

CHAPTER 3

VIRTUAL LEARNING ENVIRONMENTS (VLA) AND THEIR ASSIMILATION

The use of new educational technologies should offer the possibility of constantly reformulating courses and monitoring student learning. In addition, this reformulation contributes to changing the andragogical practices used by teaching staff. Learning through virtual environments is already a reality in a number of educational institutions.

As Jonassen (2007) put it, the teaching-learning process for acquiring knowledge in traditional education reflects an objectivist, memorist education in which instruction is used to transmit knowledge without authentic, replicable experiences, i.e. not applicable within a context. For the author, knowledge should be stimulated from a constructivist perspective, using dialogues and provoking interactions with oneself and with others. Thus, Jonassen mentions that constructivism is a learning philosophy that provides collaborative means and supports authentic experiences in the acquisition of knowledge, favouring the characteristics of the distance learning environment.

However, Jonassen (2007) points out that distance education has used technology to replace live, face-to-face instruction, but has often repeated the most ineffective instructional methods of traditional education. For the author, the use of technology in education will only be considered innovative if there are changes in educational paradigms.

In recent decades, Litto (2009) has pointed out that there have been significant changes in Brazilian educational institutions and society. The industrial society, centred on work, which prioritised teaching, has been suppressed by a new concept, called the information or network society, which focuses on learning. In the network society, the education process is mediated by information and communication technologies. The roles of the actors change: the teacher is the mediator and the student is active in the construction of knowledge (LITTO, 2009).

3.1 Characteristics of the new environment

The implementation and sharing of a single VLE by the schools brought major challenges in meeting the demands of all the schools, which in turn had their own specific needs and methodology. It was also a great opportunity to review existing processes and improve them, so it was possible to highlight the strengths of each reality and apply them to the new project.

For the most part, the process of creating courses and enrolments used to be done through daily uploads, which required manual intervention and caused problems due to inconsistent information or *delays*. With the new VLE, uploads are now carried out automatically and periodically, consuming information directly from the academic registration system, enabling a single authentication standard.

The new VLE has a much more intuitive interface for teachers and students to navigate and use the available resources. The organisation of the interface makes it easier to understand the existing modules and resources. This opinion was shared with the CTE team at each of the face-to-face meetings. It was possible to create a visual identity that respected the characteristics of each school, such as colour, typography, shapes, logos and so on. The big gain was that every school was able to have its own visual identity by applying automatic customisation without manual intervention.

In order to include all possible audiences, care was taken to ensure that the new VLE accepted web accessibility standards, i.e. it was compatible with assistive technologies such as screen readers, which facilitates navigation and understanding.

Uploading documents is a common feature in VLEs, but the difference is the plagiarism check. This feature supports the teacher in measuring student commitment and the authenticity of the activities handed in, reducing the incidents of unoriginal work over time.

The management part of the system is more flexible compared to previous VLEs and allows for greater customisation and control by administrators in such a way as not to compromise the core of the VLE, i.e. altering its source code. This is very important for FGV, as it is necessary to guarantee a certain amount of autonomy and freedom for each of the eight schools.

Despite these important contributions with the implementation of the new AVA, it is well known that there are still a number of improvements to be made, such as the fact that there is no integration between the academic registration system (SRA) and the AVA. As there is no integration between the systems, lecturers have to enter grades and absences in the SRA system and publish content and activities in the AVA, forcing lecturers to access two different environments.

This is the kind of improvement that, if made, would be of great benefit to teachers, as this is a common complaint from teachers when face-to-face training sessions are held.

CHAPTER 4

THE RESEARCH

In order to identify the level of use of the ECLASS platform and the critical points that lead to non-adherence by a portion of professors, a survey was carried out based on the questionnaire attached to this document and sent to the total population of professors at FGV, at its various educational levels (undergraduate, postgraduate, master's, doctorate and extension courses) and schools (CPDOC, Direito RJ, Direito SP, EAESP, EBAPE, EESP, EMAP and EPGE).

The survey was sent to 835 teachers, 150, 18.0% of whom actually answered all the questions. The sample used for this analysis, however, included 148 teachers, as two respondents were disregarded due to inconsistencies in the Age and Length of Service fields.

4.1 The results

The responses analysed are distributed as follows between the FGV schools (Graph 9) and the course/programme in which the professor currently teaches (Graph 10):

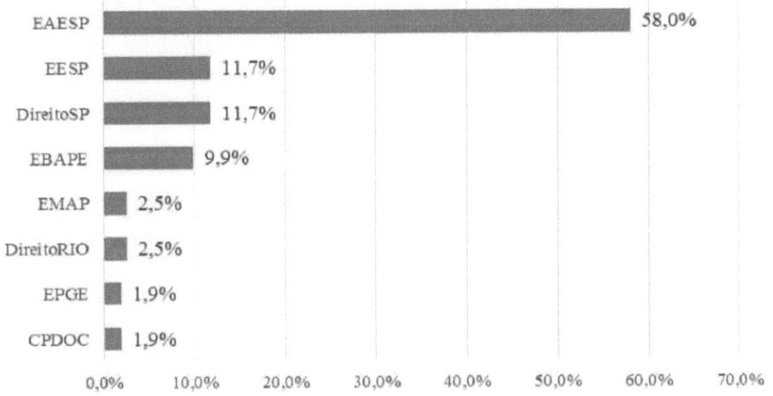

Graph 10 - Percentage share of teachers who responded to the survey by schools where they currently teach.

Source: author's elaboration

These results indicate that the majority of the survey respondents were professors who teach at schools located in São Paulo and at FGV's undergraduate and postgraduate programmes. The strong participation of teachers from the São Paulo School of Business Administration (EAESP) is noteworthy.

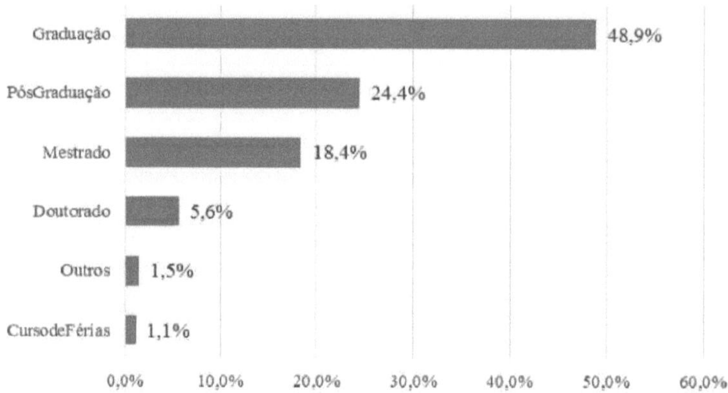

Graph 11 - Percentage share of teachers who responded to the survey by programme in which they currently teach.

Source: author's elaboration

When we consider the age reported by the respondents, we see that the majority of these teachers, corresponding to 53.4% of the total, are between 41 and 60 years old. It is worth noting, however, that 19.6 per cent of respondents are in the 60+ age bracket, which reveals a significant engagement of teachers who are older and therefore closer to retirement. In addition, the high average age of the professors is in line with the excellence in teaching promoted by FGV, which prioritises hiring professors with PhDs and extensive experience in the professional market.

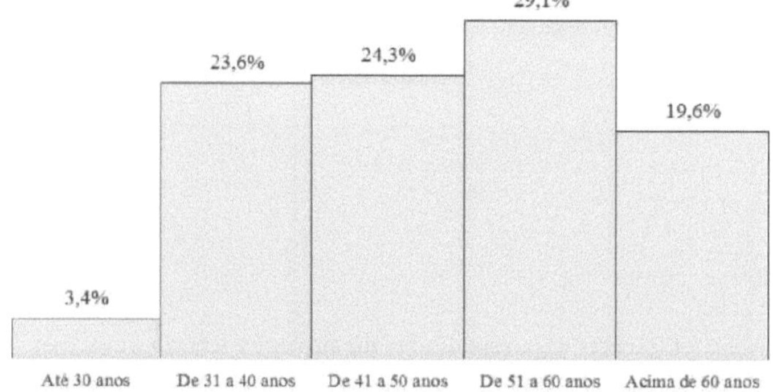

Graph 12 - Percentage share of teachers who responded to the survey by age group.

Source: author's elaboration

A curious fact about the survey is that most of the teaching staff who took part in the questionnaire have only been teaching at FGV for a few years. Almost 37 per cent of respondents said they had been teaching for less than five years at the schools listed in the questionnaire, and 54.1 per cent said they had been at FGV for less than 10 years.

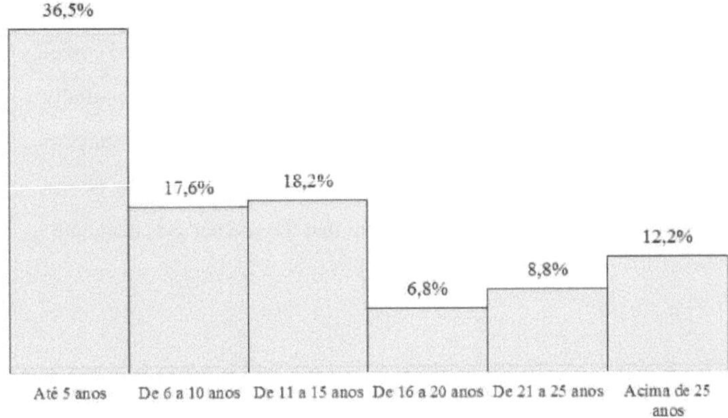

Graph 13 - Percentage share of teachers who responded to the survey by length of service.

Source: author's elaboration.

With regard to the use of the ECLASS platform, it is interesting to note that only a minority of the teaching staff included in the survey do not use the tool. Out of a total of 148 responses, only 8 teachers said they didn't use the platform, while another 78 teachers said they used it more than once a week. In other words, although it exists, non-adherence to the platform is low.

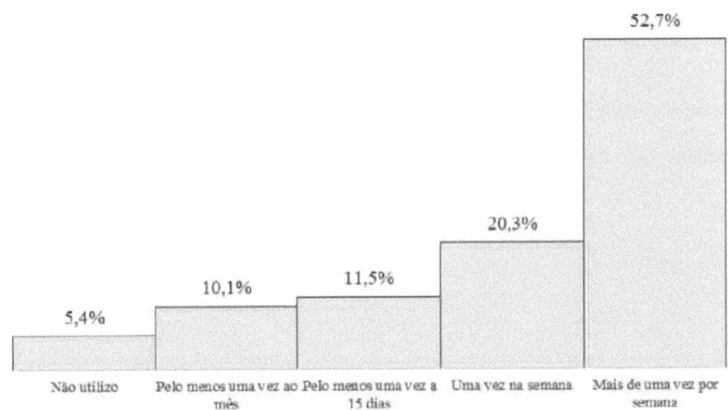

Graph 14 - Frequency of use of ECLASS by the teachers taking part in the survey.
Source: author's elaboration.

It should be borne in mind, however, that this result refers to the sample studied and does not necessarily reflect the frequency of use of the platform by the entire FGV teaching staff. Despite the high frequency of use of the platform, few teachers use all of the 14 functionalities described in the questionnaire. The majority work with only 3 of these functionalities and just over 90% of respondents use up to 6 of them. It is also worth noting that the platform is not considered complex to use by the majority of teaching staff, as more than 40 per cent of respondents fully or partially disagreed with the statement that ECLASS is not easy to use. There also don't seem to be any significant complaints about a lack of support for using the platform, since approximately 60 per cent of those surveyed fully or partially agreed with the statement that the teacher gets adequate support for its use.

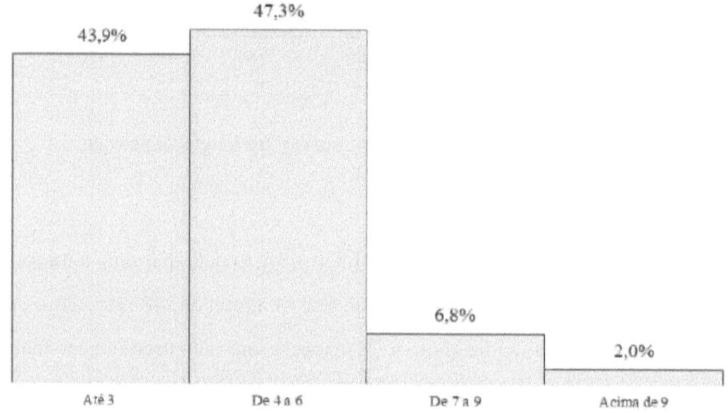

Graph 15 - Number of ECLASS functionalities used by the teachers taking part in the survey. Source: author's elaboration.

Finally, the survey data seems to corroborate the general assessment that ECLASS is beneficial in supporting face-to-face classes. In fact, few teachers disagreed with this statement: only 31 teachers.

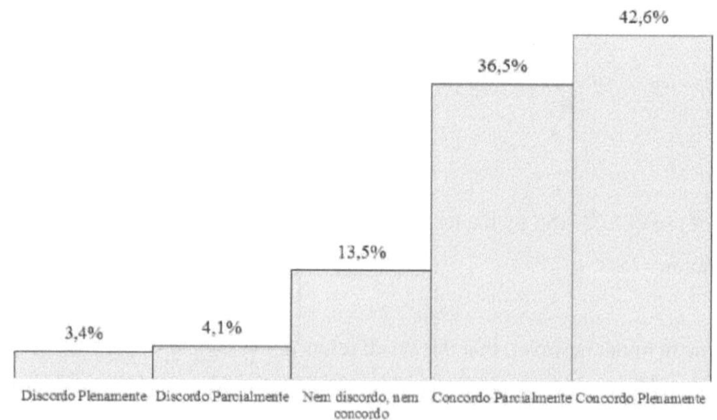

Graph 16 - Percentage share of responses to the statement that ECLASS is beneficial in supporting face-to-face classes.

Source: author's elaboration.

CHAPTER 5

STATISTICAL ANALYSIS

As discussed above, the aim of this work is to analyse the level of use of the ECLASS platform, as well as to identify the critical points that lead to non-adherence by a proportion of FGV teachers.

From the sample available, *it* can be seen that 27% of the teachers surveyed hardly use the platform. In other words, 40 of the 148 teachers who responded to the survey said that they don't use ECLASS or that they use it less than once a week.

Based on these figures, hypotheses were verified to understand why this portion of the teaching staff does not use the platform. By comparing the information on the frequency of use of ECLASS with the other data provided by the teachers, a search will be made to find answers to this question.

5.1 Older teachers may use ECLASS less

The first hypothesis to be tested asks whether the age reported by teachers is directly related to how often they use ECLASS. That is, whether teachers who are older than the rest tend to use the platform less. This hypothesis assumes that younger teachers tend to be more interested in using the latest technologies, as they are more integrated into modern procedures for supporting face-to-face lessons and communicating with students. The hypothesis also assumes that older teachers may prefer traditional methods to modern teaching tools.

To obtain an answer to this question, the age variable was linked, defined as an age group with a ten-year interval between each category, and the variable of frequency of use of ECLASS, which asks the respondent to choose between the following options which best suits their usage profile: I don't use it, I use it at least once a month, at least once every fortnight, once a week or twice a week.

However, the results show that there is no relationship between these two variables. In fact, the average age calculated for teachers who use the platform little does not differ statistically from the average age of teachers who say they use ECLASS at least once a week. As the table below shows, the standard deviation of the answers also differed little between the two groups.

Table 7 - Relationship between Age Group and Frequency of Use of ECLASS

Age group	Do not use or use little		They use it often	
	Frequency (ni)	Relative Frequency	Frequency (ni)	Relative Frequency

		(fi)		(fi)
Up to 30 years old	2	5,0%	3	2,8%
31 to 40 years old	11	27,5%	24	22,2%
From 41 to 50 years old	7	17,5%	29	26,9%
From 51 to 60 years old	11	27,5%	32	29,6%
Over 60	9	22,5%	20	18,5%
Grand Total	**40**	**100%**	**108**	**100%**

Source: Questionnaire sent to FGV professors. Own elaboration.

Table 8 - Relationship between Age Group and Frequency of Use of ECLASS

Frequency of use E-Class	Age group		
	Average	Variance	Deviate Pattern
Do not use or use little	49.00	152,75	12.36
They use it often	49,39	121,91	11,04

Source: Questionnaire sent to FGV professors. Own elaboration.

This assessment is further supported by the fact that the correlation between the two variables is very low, statistically non-existent. The joint distribution of the variables, shown in the contingency table below, and the calculated correlation coefficient of approximately 0.6 per cent, show how strong the evidence is that there is no direct relationship between the age group of teachers and the frequency of use of ECLASS.

Table 9 - Joint distribution of Age Group and Frequency of ECLASS use

Age group	Frequency of use of the E-Class					Grand Total
	I don't use it	Peb at least once a month	At least once every 15 days	Once a week	More than once a week	
Up to 30 years old	0,0%	0,0%	1,4%	0,0%	2,0%	**3,4%**
31 to 40 years old	2,0%	4,1%	1,4%	4,1%	12,2%	**23,6%**
From 41 to 50 years old	0,0%	2,0%	2,7%	6,1%	13,5%	**24,3%**
From 51 to 60 years old	2,0%	2,0%	3,4%	7,4%	14,2%	**29,1%**
Over 60	1,4%	2,0%	2,7%	2,7%	10,8%	**19,6%**
Grand Total	**5,4%**	**10,1%**	**11,5%**	**20,3%**	**52,7%**	**100,0%**
					fndice of Correlation:	0,646%

Source: Questionnaire sent to FGV professors. Own elaboration.

5.2 Teachers with more time on the job may use ECLASS less

After rejecting the first hypothesis, we will assess whether the frequency of use of ECLASS is related not to the teacher's age, but to their length of service, i.e. the total number of years they have been teaching at FGV up to the present time. This time, the hypothesis assumes that teachers who have worked at FGV for longer would be more resistant to repeated changes in the platforms that support face-to-face classes and would therefore stop using the most recent tool. Firstly, however, it was considered very important to test how the length of service reported by the teachers surveyed relates to age. Another hypothesis was that the amount of time spent at home is directly proportional to the age of each teacher and, as such, the result of the previous question would tend to be little different from that observed for the relationship between age and use of ECLASS.

In fact, the combination of teachers' length of service and their respective years of life shows a direct positive relationship between these two variables. The arrangement of the dots in graph 16 shows that the older the teacher, the longer they have been at home. The correlation index between these two pieces of information is close to 68 per cent.

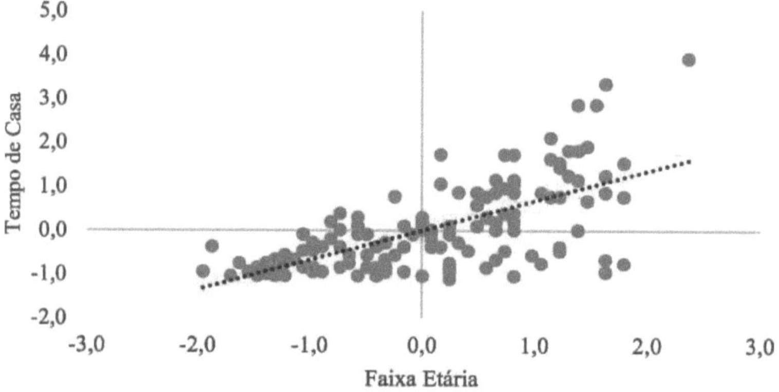

Graph 17 - Relationship between Age Group and Time at Home (standardised indices).
Source: author's elaboration.

It is therefore to be expected that the second hypothesis worked on, the one linking non-use of ECLASS with teachers' length of service, will also be rejected. In order to measure the relationship between the frequency of use of ECLASS and length of service, we distributed this information in bands with a five-year interval between each category.

Table 10 - Relationship between Time at Home and Frequency of Use of ECLASS

Length of service (in years)	**Do not use or use little**		**They use it often**	
	Frequency (ni)	Frequency Relative (fi)	Frequency (ni)	Relative Frequency (fi)
Up to 5 years	20	50,0%	34	31,5%
From 6 to 10 years old	5	12,5%	21	19,4%
From 11 to 15 years old	7	17,5%	20	18,5%
From 16 to 20 years old	2	5,0%	8	7,4%
21 to 25 years old	1	2,5%	12	11,1%
Over 25 years old	5	12,5%	13	12,0%
Grand Total	**40**	**100%**	**108**	**100%**

Table 11 - Relationship between Time at Home and Frequency of Use of ECLASS

Frequency of use of the E-Class	Age group		
	Average	Variance	Standard Deviation
Do not use or use little	9,75	74,44	8,63
They use it often	12,17	75,69	8,70

5.3 Teachers with more time on the job are also older teachers.

As with the previous relationship, the average home time of teachers who use the platform little does not differ statistically from the average of teachers who said they use ECLASS at least once a week. The correlation index calculated, although higher than the result found for the first situation, is also very low and does not allow for the assertion that the longer the teacher's home time, the less willing they are to use the platform. The positive value of the index, and also the differences between the averages, could still suggest that the relationship is contrary to what was hypothesised. However, the result of close to 13 per cent is still considered statistically weak and does not allow this statement to be accepted.

Table 12 - Joint distribution of Time at Home and Frequency of ECLASS use

Home Time	Frequency of use of the E-Class					Grand Total
	I don't use it	At least once a month	I breastfeed at least once every fortnight	Once a week	More than once a week	
Up to 5 years	2,0%	5,4%	6,1%	7,4%	15,5%	**36,5%**
From 6 to 10 years old	1,4%	1,4%	0,7%	3,4%	10,8%	**17,6%**
From 11 to 15 years old	0,0%	2,7%	2,0%	4,7%	8,8%	**18,2%**
From 16 to 20 years old	0,7%	0,7%	0,0%	0,7%	4,7%	**6,8%**
21 to 25 years old	0,0%	0,0%	0,7%	3,4%	4,7%	**8,8%**
Over 25 years old	1,4%	0,0%	2,0%	0,7%	8,1%	**12,2%**
Grand Total	**5,4%**	**10,1%**	**11,5%**	**20,3%**	**52,7%**	**100,0%**
					Correlation index:	**13,134%**

5.4 The lack of take-up and under-utilisation may have been due to a lack of communication and publicity about the platform and its benefits

Having rejected these two hypotheses, the information that best helps to explain why a portion of FGV teachers did not sign up to ECLASS is the teachers' perception of the benefit provided by the platform in supporting face-to-face classes. Communication and publicising of the platform may not have reached all teachers, which may have influenced their perception of the real benefits of ECLASS in their day-to-day work.

In fact, unlike what happened with the two previous hypotheses, it is possible to see from the information obtained from cross-referencing the benefit perceived by the teacher in using ECLASS and the frequency of use of this tool, that these two variables are directly related to each other. Teachers who do not perceive the benefits of ECLASS tend not to use the tool. Or, the less the teacher perceives the benefits of the tool, the less they use it.

In order to identify each teacher's perception of the benefits of the platform, the questionnaire asked the respondent to list their level of agreement with the following statement on a scale from 1 (strongly disagree) to 5 (strongly agree): "In your opinion, does the ECLASS system provide benefits in supporting your classroom lessons?".

Table 13 - Joint distribution of Perceived benefits of ECLASS and Frequency of use

0 Does E-Class benefit classroom teaching?	Frequency of use of the E-Class					Grand Total
	I don't use it	At least once a month	At least once every 15 days	Once a week	More than once a week	
I strongly disagree	1,4%	0,0%	0,7%	0,0%	1,4%	**3,4%**
I disagree	0,0%	2,0%	0,0%	1,4%	0,7%	**4,1%**
Neither disagree nor agree	2,7%	1,4%	2,7%	4,1%	2,7%	**13,5%**
I agree	0,7%	5,4%	2,7%	6,1%	21,6%	**36,5%**
I totally agree	0,7%	1,4%	5,4%	8,8%	26,4%	**42,6%**
Grand Total	**5,4%**	**10,1%**	**11,5%**	**20,3%**	**52,7%**	**100,0%**

Correlation index: 34,809%

Source: Questionnaire sent to FGV professors. Own elaboration.

5.5 The perception of benefits is directly related to teachers' awareness of existing functionalities

If not realising the benefits that ECLASS brings to face-to-face classes is one of the factors that help explain why teachers don't sign up to the platform, what would lead them not to identify the platform's positive points? With the information obtained in the survey and based on the data sample provided, a strong relationship was found between the teachers' opinion of ECLASS and their awareness of the functionalities available on the platform.

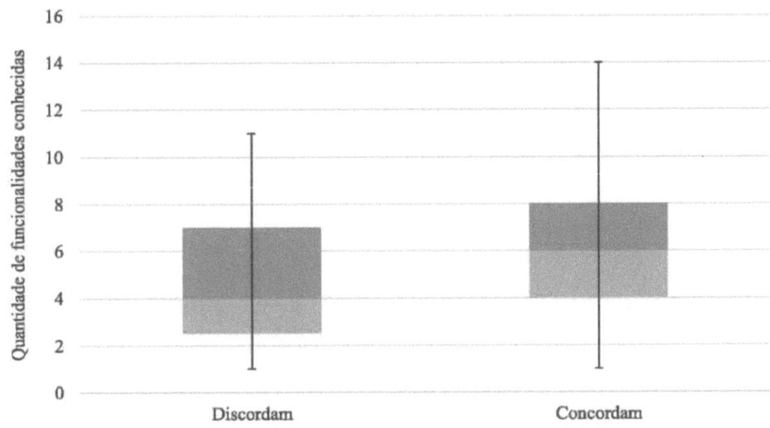

Graph 18 - Number of functionalities known by teachers per agreement group in relation to the benefit of ECLASS in supporting face-to-face classes

Source: author's elaboration.

The lower the knowledge of ECLASS functionalities, the greater the disagreement with the statement that ECLASS brings benefits to the classroom.

Table 14 - Joint distribution of Perceived benefits of ECLASS and Number of known functionalities

Number of functionalities the teacher is aware of	Does E-Class bring benefits to face-to-face classes?					Grand Total
	I strongly disagree	Partially disagree	Neither disagree nor agree	Partially agree	I totally agree	
1	1,4%	0,7%	2,0%	1,4%	0,7%	6,1%
2	0,0%	0,7%	0,7%	1,4%	0,7%	3,4%
3	1,4%	0,0%	3,4%	0,7%	6,8%	12,2%
4	0,7%	0,0%	1,4%	8,1%	4,7%	14,9%
5	0,0%	0,7%	0,0%	6,1%	4,7%	11,5%
6	0,0%	0,0%	2,0%	6,1%	6,1%	14,2%
7	0,0%	0,7%	0,7%	1,4%	1,4%	4,1%
8	0,0%	0,7%	1,4%	2,7%	6,8%	11,5%
9	0,0%	0,7%	0,0%	2,0%	4,1%	6,8%
10	0,0%	0,0%	1,4%	1,4%	2,0%	4,7%
11	0,0%	0,0%	0,7%	0,7%	2,0%	3,4%
12	0,0%	0,0%	0,0%	1,4%	2,0%	3,4%
13	0,0%	0,0%	0,0%	2,0%	0,7%	2,7%
14	0,0%	0,0%	0,0%	1,4%	0,0%	1,4%
Grand Total	3,4%	4,1%	13,5%	36,5%	42,6%	100,0%
					Correlation index:	23,824%

This information corroborates the hypothesis that communication may have failed to reach the entire FGV teaching staff.

5.6 Teachers from a particular school may use ECLASS less

It was also found that the distribution between schools of teachers who make little use of ECLASS is more heterogeneous than the distribution between the 148 teachers as a whole, which allows us to infer that this possible communication failure was not an isolated case at a particular FGV school.

CHAPTER 6

PROPOSAL

As a proposal, actions will be taken, which will be duly described in this chapter, with the aim of reducing the non-adherence of FGV teachers from 31 per cent of teachers to 11 per cent. This reduction will take place over one year, starting in January 2018 and ending in January 2019. After this action has been completed, a new survey will be carried out in order to once again measure the rate at which FGV lecturers have signed up to the new VLE, and then check whether the actions taken over the year have been successful in achieving a reduction in non-adherence.

6.1 Exploratory Research

In order to choose which actions should be taken to reduce the non-adherence rate to 11 per cent and be more effective, assertive and efficient, an exploratory survey was carried out with a sample of the teachers who make up the universe of those who have not adhered to the new VLE.

It is worth emphasising that exploratory research, according to Gil (1999), aims to provide a general overview of a particular fact.

A sample of 10 per cent of the 27 per cent of teachers surveyed who make little use of the platform was therefore taken. In other words, 4 teachers were selected out of the 40 who responded to the survey and stated that they do not use ECLASS.

In order to provide a general overview of the fact, the research carried out in person consisted of answering the following questions:

1- How does the teacher teach his or her class, in other words, what dynamics does he or she use?

2- What are your interaction needs with students? For example, do you need to communicate outside of class, share material or carry out activities?

3- Do you already use any technological resources in your classes? If yes, which ones? If not, for what reason?

4- Is the teacher familiar with ECLASS? If so, have they used it? If not, why not?

6.2 Answers from the Exploratory Survey

In order to preserve the identity of the teachers who took part in this research, their details and any information that might imply their identification will be concealed.

The first teacher to take part in the survey is 72 years old and has been teaching subjects at the School of Economics and Business Administration for over 35 years.

At the moment, teachers use lectures, the dynamics of which boil down to explaining the theory, giving concrete examples and problems to be solved in the classroom, after which similar problems must be done outside of class and if there are any doubts, the student must explain them in class.

In order to share the material used by the teacher, which is often a power point presentation, as well as the activities to be carried out, the teacher asks the students to buy a set of printed sheets from the FGV bookshop.

There are two major needs for this teacher:

- Sharing the material used in class e;
- Sharing maths exercises for students to do, both in class and afterwards.

The teacher reported that he doesn't use any technology apart from the computer and the Datashow in the classroom.

When asked about ECLASS, the teacher said that he was familiar with it, but had never used it because he didn't believe it could bring great benefits to his class, because, for example, for classes where there is a need to carry out exercises in class, when students buy the recommended material the teacher guarantees that everyone will have the necessary material at the moment, but if he puts the exercises on ECLASS, perhaps not all students will bring a device to the classroom to access them, or perhaps the student won't print out the necessary sheets.

It was proposed to the teacher that he initially publish his power point presentations on ECLASS, as this would guarantee that all students would have access, as well as avoiding waste, since the set of sheets that were made available in the bookshop was printed before we even knew how many students there would be in each class, as well as having the benefit of making any changes to the presentation without the need to repress.

The teacher was shown the quiz feature with automatic correction, so the teacher could create all the exercises in this feature and the students could do the maths and choose the result from a number of options, as well as setting the availability date and execution time. The system corrects automatically and automatic feedback can be configured according to the answer chosen by the student. When the teacher learnt about this feature, he commented that it would be of great value, as it would save a lot of time when correcting exercises, but he claimed that there would still be the problem that not all students would bring devices to class that allowed access to ECLASS. To resolve this issue, it was suggested that the labs be used for the classes where the students would do the exercises, or that the Audio Visual Centre (CAV) be asked to provide laptops in the classroom for those days.

The second teacher is 38 years old and has been at FGV for just under a year. In his classes he uses a lot of videos from the internet, power point presentations and articles, news and printed texts to read in class to stimulate discussion. He has a need to share the materials he teaches.

The teacher does not use any technology other than what is present in the classroom, which is the computer and Datashow. The teacher claimed that some students had spoken to him about ECLASS, but he didn't know what the platform was for, he knew about other school systems such as the online teacher, but not ECLASS.

This teacher was shown some of ECLASS's resources, such as the content area where he could publish all the materials shown in class. The teacher was also instructed to use the *flip class* methodology, also known as the inverted classroom, in which students are asked some questions before the class takes place, generating doubt and the need to research, with the student being encouraged to prepare better before the class even takes place. ECLASS supports the use of this methodology, because in the case of this teacher, he will publish in advance the texts that were read in class, so that the student can read them before the class, allowing the time in class to be better utilised and the discussions to be richer.

The teacher said that the methodology was good, but there was no guarantee that the students would actually read the texts. As a solution, it was proposed that the teacher create a quiz in ECLASS with some questions about the proposed text and link some punctuation to it, so that the students are motivated to read the texts and check their understanding when they complete the quiz.

Once the suggestions had been made, the teacher agreed to use ECLASS if he had the necessary support.

The third professor is 55 years old and has been teaching at the Getulio Vargas Foundation in the School of Law for around 10 years. His classes are usually a mix of lectures and dialogues. It's worth remembering that in dialogues, the teacher encourages the student to take a less passive stance by introducing questions for the students to answer, making the classroom activity more dynamic.

This teacher needs to communicate, both to send notices of upcoming activities that may change according to changes in the political landscape, as well as notices of important events that are taking place, and also in order to encourage discussion outside the classroom.

The teacher uses email and whatsapp for all communication, but said that it would be very interesting to have a feature where he and his students could rate or classify their colleagues' comments, as well as having a single place where messages could be organised by topic. The teacher said that he was familiar with the old version of ECLASS, and that in the distant past, about seven years ago, he used the old version, but wasn't interested in the new version because he couldn't see any benefit other than publishing his material.

In order to meet the needs reported by the teacher, it was proposed that, as well as publishing the materials in the content resource, the teacher should use the discussion forum resource, so that the teacher can create forums according to each discussion topic, thus making the environment more organised. What's more, the teacher can set an availability date for participation in the discussions and after that date the forum will only be available for consultation. It is also possible to evaluate and classify each student's comments as a ranking, i.e. each student can rate their comments up to 5 stars and the best rated comments are highlighted.

Another resource allied to this teacher's need is the e-mail option in ECLASS. By sending a message using ECLASS's internal feature, students are notified via their private e-mail address, as well as being notified when they access the platform, i.e. if their private e-mail address happens to be full, or is registered incorrectly, when the student accesses the platform they will be able to view the teacher's message.

The fourth and final teacher to take part in the exploratory research is 66 years old and has been teaching at a history school in Rio de Janeiro for around 15 years. The dynamics of his classes are expository, with the teacher discussing a topic using a pen and whiteboard. The teacher doesn't use any kind of technological support.

The teacher needs to share the material used in class and receive the students' activities, which are often texts on a specific history topic. The students hand in these printed texts in class for the teacher to correct. As mentioned above, the teacher doesn't use any technology to support his lessons. The teacher has heard of ECLASS, but has never used it because he doesn't feel confident in using the technology and doesn't know what resources it has.

The teacher was shown the content area so that he can publish all his classroom materials on ECLASS. He was also shown the dropbox feature that allows students to send their texts to the teacher, with the possibility of automatic checking and plagiarism. The teacher was also pleased to learn that it is possible to correct and give feedback to students via audio and video, which would save a lot of time when correcting texts.

6.3 Actions of the proposal

Analysing the answers from the exploratory survey, it was possible to conclude that the four teachers interviewed did not use ECLASS because they were unaware of the benefits it could bring to their classes. This information once again corroborates the hypothesis that communication has failed to reach FGV's teaching staff in its entirety.

Following this conclusion, it is necessary to take actions that can change this situation and achieve the goal of reducing non-adherence among FGV teachers from 31 per cent to 11 per cent.

The first action to be taken will be the creation of video pills that will be sent by e-mail to teachers, as well as being made available on the ECLASS login page on a monthly basis.

The content of the video clips will be to present cases of teachers' daily difficulties and how ECLASS can help to solve or improve the situation, such as the case of the fourth teacher in the survey, where the difficulty of organising all the work received in print, the lack of checking for plagiarism and how to save time when correcting work is reported.

Another action will be to organise events with the Foundation's teachers. Key teachers who make continuous and efficient use of the platform will be identified and will be able to share their experiences with other colleagues. These teachers will be knowledge multipliers. The multiplier teachers will show their colleagues the success stories they have had using ECLASS to support their classroom lessons. This event will also publicise the new resources and their possible uses, provide an overview of existing resources, publicise the CTE area and the support available for using ECLASS. Two dates will be set for next year, and prices are already being quoted for coffee breaks, kits to be delivered at the event and the booking of the auditorium. The event should take place in about two hours so as not to take up the scarce time that teachers have.

Formal communications will be made containing information in the form of infographics with important figures on the use of ECLASS by each school and each programme, and will take place every six months. The communications will be sent to each respective school headmaster and programme coordinator. It is believed that with this action, headmasters and coordinators will be able to monitor the actual use of ECLASS and, if necessary, they will be able to encourage use from the top down, i.e. when they notice that use by teachers of the programme for which the coordinator is responsible is low, they will be able to ask them why, and work will be done with the coordinators to keep the team responsible for ECLASS informed of feedback from teachers in order to act on critical points. Note that there is an assumption that headmasters and coordinators will be allies of the team responsible for ECLASS because they believe in the benefits that ECLAS can bring to their teachers' classes.

The provision of training in the use of ECLASS resources is another action that will be carried out on a monthly basis. Teachers will be encouraged to contact the team responsible for ECLASS to book a training session. Unlike in the past, this offer will take place on an individual basis. It's worth remembering that when the new ECLASS was implemented, several group training sessions were held. In the current scenario, in which ECLASS is more widespread and the 30 per cent of teachers who have not yet joined need to be heard, so that there is a deeper understanding of their needs and specificities.

In addition, a mapping of how teachers are hired at the Getulio Vargas Foundation's eight schools will be carried out.

With the mapping carried out, it will be possible to approach teachers right at the start of their activities, thus being able to offer and present the full potential of the AVA, as well as present them with a "welcome" kit in which the benefits of using ECLASS as an extension of the classroom are emphasised.

6.4 Action schedule

Below is a timetable of actions to be taken by the Educational Technology Coordination, which is the area responsible for the virtual learning environment, ECLASS, in order to alleviate non-adherence by a portion of the Getulio Vargas Foundation's teaching staff:

Table 15 - Timetable - Actions to achieve the target of reducing non-adherence by FGV teachers

Activities	January	February	March	April	May	June	July	August	September	October	November	December	January 2019
Timetable - Actions to achieve the goal of reducing non-adherence by FGV teachers													
1® Action - Video Pills													
Preparation of video pill scripts	X												
Creating video pills	X		X				X		X		X		
Publicising the video pill	X		X				X		X		X		
2nd Action - Event with teachers													
Event planning				X	X								
Review the first plan										X	X		
Organisation of the event						X						X	
Action 3 - Normal communications													
Planning the layout, template and information to be included in the reports		X											
Data collection and production of the press release					X						X		

Release of the statement														
4th Action - Offering training														
Publicising the possibility of individual training														
			5th Action - Approach to teachers on admission										
Mapping the hiring process														
Preparation of the approach to teachers and the welcome kit														
6th Action - Evaluating the results achieved with actions taken														
Collection of ECLASS usage data														
Presentation of the final result														
Caption														

Forecast   Realised   Not realised   Reproduction

Source: author's elaboration.

CHAPTER 7

CONCLUSION

Based on the responses of 148 teachers from the Getulio Vargas Foundation to the questionnaire that was carried out in order to find satisfactory explanations to the questions listed in the objective of this work, it was concluded that the teachers who make little use of the ECLASS system represent a minority within the total number of respondents to the survey.

Despite this, it was possible to identify one main reason, among the variables studied in this study, as a motivating factor for the small number of teachers not having signed up to the new platform.

Cross-referencing the answers regarding the frequency of use of ECLASS with the other information provided by the teachers, followed by a statistical analysis of how the variables related to each other, allowed the rejection of common hypotheses to explain non-adherence to the tool (such as age and length of service) and identified the low perception of the benefits of ECLASS by some teachers as the main determinant of the low use of the digital platform.

It was possible to distinguish that teachers who use ECLASS little tend not to realise the benefits that the platform provides in supporting face-to-face classes. It was noted that the lack of perception is directly related to the number of features of the ECLASS system that teachers are aware of.

Therefore, what the sample allows us to say is that the less teachers know about the functionalities of the ECLASS system, the less they perceive the benefits that the platform can offer to support face-to-face classes and, therefore, the less frequently teachers use ECLASS.

The above statements could be verified when the exploratory survey was applied to a sample of four specific teachers who made up the universe of teachers who had not signed up to ECLASS. As the survey showed, the majority of teachers did not use ECLASS because they were unaware of its benefits.

Following these findings, suggestions were made for more efficient actions to reduce non-adherence among FGV teachers from 31 per cent to 11 per cent in one year.

These actions should reach all of FGV's teaching staff, regardless of the school where they work, as no significant differences were found in the distribution of teachers who make little use of the platform between FGV's various schools compared to those who use it at least once a week. These actions should clearly present the benefits of using ECLASS to support face-to-face classes.

REFERENCES

ARVAN, Lanny: Dis-Integrating the LMS. Educause Quarterly. vol. 32, no. 2, 2009.

CARVALHO, Silvio. Quality dimensions in virtual learning environments. Doctoral Thesis in Business Administration, University of São Paulo, FEA-USP, 2009.

CUBAN, Larry: Oversold and Underused: Computers in the Classroom. Harvard University Press, Cambridge, MA, pp. 129,138,2001.

GIL, Antonio. Methods and techniques of social research. São Paulo: Atlas, 1999.

JONASSEN, D. Computers, Cognitive Tools: developing critical thinking in schools. Porto-Portugal: Porto Editora. 21st Century Educational Sciences Collection, no. 23, 2007.

LANE, Lisa. Insidious Pedagogy: How Course Management Systems Impact Pedagogy. First Monday, vol. 14, no. 10, 2009.

KNOWLES, Malcolm: the adult student. A neglected species. 4ª ed. Houston: Gulf Publishing, 1973.

LAKATOS, Eva Maria; MARCONI, Marina de Andrade: Fundamentals of Scientific Methodology. Atlas Editora, 2010.

LITTO, F. FORMIGA, M. Educação a Distância: o estado da arte. São Paulo: Pearson Education do Brasil, 2009.

LUNA, Sérgio Vasconcelos. Research planning: an introduction. São Paulo: EDUC, 1997.

MARTINS, Gilberto de Andrade; DOMINGUES, Osmar: General and Applied Statistics. Atlas Editora, 2014, 5ª edition.

RESEARCH METHODOLOGY - available at: https://pt.wikipedia.Org/wiki/Metodologia_de_pesquisa_estat%C3%ADstica#Vis.C3.A3o_Ge ral. Accessed on: 15/05/2017.

PORTAL FGV - available at: http://portal.fgv.br/sites/portal.fgv.br/files/u90/annual_2016_versao_digital.pdf. Accessed on: 20/09/2017

PORTAL DA EDUCAÇÃO - available at:

http://www.portaleducacao.com.br/administracao/artigos/49547/estatistica-qualitativa-e-quantitative#ixzz49FvZ9rWt. Accessed on: 12/09/2017

RUMSEY, Deborah: Statistics for Dummies. Starlin Alpha Publishing, 2009.

U.S. Department of Education. Hamessing Innovation to Support Student Success: Using Technology to Personalise Education. p. 9, 2008.

yes
I want morebooks!

Buy your books fast and straightforward online - at one of world's fastest growing online book stores! Environmentally sound due to Print-on-Demand technologies.

Buy your books online at
www.morebooks.shop

Kaufen Sie Ihre Bücher schnell und unkompliziert online – auf einer der am schnellsten wachsenden Buchhandelsplattformen weltweit! Dank Print-On-Demand umwelt- und ressourcenschonend produzi ert.

Bücher schneller online kaufen
www.morebooks.shop